Free of the Shadow

poems and stories

Lou Faber

Plain View Press
1101 W 34th Street, STE 404

www.plainviewpress.com
Austin, TX 78705

Copyright © 2025 Lou Faber. All rights reserved under International and Pan-American Copyright Conventions. No part of this book may be reproduced or distributed in any form or by any means, or stored in a data base or retrieval system, without written permission. All rights, including electronic, are reserved by the author and publicsher.

ISBN: 978-1-63210-107-5
Library of Congress Control Number: 2025933420

Cover art by Lou Faber
Cover design by Pam Knight

We Find Healing In Existing Reality

Plain View Press is a 47-year-old issue-based literary publishing house. Our books result from artistic collaboration between writers, artists, and editors. Over the years we have become a far-flung community of humane and highly creative activists whose energies bring humanitarian enlightenment and hope to individuals and communities grappling with the major issues of our time—peace, justice, the environment, education and gender.

Free of the Shadow

poems and stories

Lou Faber

Acknowledgements

Grateful acknowledgements are due to the editors of the following publications where these poems first appeared:
"On Buddha" in *Amethyst Review*; "In Silence" in *As Above, So Below*; "Hillel at the Golden Dragon " in *Atlanta Review*; "The Perfect Crime" in *Bakunawa Press*; "Into the Darkness" and "Morning Song" in *Cantos*; "The Paper" in *Cleaning Up Glitter*; "Rising Time" in *Compass Rose Literary Journal*; "A Moment" in *Constellations, A Journal of Poetry*; "Clockwork" in *EKL Review*; "Cabernet," "Still Mourning," "A Trois," and "The Final Scene" in *Flora Fiction*; "Senbazuru" in *Forevermore*; "Death By Cliché" and "Beggar's Tale" in *Glimpse*; "My Judas" in *Homer's Odyssey*; "Buenos Aires on the Genessee" in *Legal Studies Forum*; "The Saint of Uncounted Names" in *Liquid Imagination*; "The Park" and "Night at the Allusive Tavern" in *Literary Odyssey*; "A Day" in *New Feathers Anthology*; "A City Out There" and "Over the Fence" in *North of Oxford*; "Reaching" in *Persephone Literary Magazine*; "October Weekend" in *Prosetrics (Rudeneja)*; "Sir, Yes Sir" and "SOS" in *Proud to Serve*; "Basho Redux" and "Broken Bow" in *Punt Volat*; "On the Shelf" in *The Birdseed*; "Quiet Departure" in *The Brussels Review*; "Upward" in *The Globe Review*; "Tokyo Night Scenes" and "Tokyo Snapshots" in *The Greyhound Journal*; "By Moonlight" in *The Seventh Quary Poetry*; "Condemned" in *These Writers' Voices*; and "Bamboo" in *The Whisky Blot*.

"Musing Tokyo" is reprinted by permission of Pussycat Press from *Around the World, Landscapes & Cityscapes*, ©2021.
"A Perfect Stillness" is reprinted by permission of The Poet, from *Culture and Identity, Vol. 2*, © 2022.
"Advice to the Young Pianist" is reprinted by permission of Pussycat Press from *Movement: Our Bodies in Action*, © 2022.
"Bandage" is reprinted by permission of Experiments In Fiction from *Anthropocene Hymnal*, © 2021.
    Several of the poems in this collection were written during my participation in the Imaginative Storm circle of writers.

To Elaine
my love, my life, my joy and my muse. She gives meaning to each day, each moment, and purpose to my life and writing. She is a woman of words and deeds, deeply compassionate, there for others in times of need. Going through life with her is a journey I never want to end. And to Teri, who is a furry bundle of joy, able to lighten even the darkest moments. She knows what I need and when I need it, and for a brushing, she will gladly give it. Finally this is for the birth mother I discovered too late, but without whom I would not be here today.

Previous Collection of Poetry
by Lou Faber

The Right to Depart: New and Selected Poems
Plain View Press (2008)
ISBN: 9780911051308, 164 pages

Contents

Acknowledgements	4

Looking Out

Morning Song	13
Advice To the Young Pianist	14
October Weekend	16
Buenos Aires on the Genessee	17
The Park	18
Cabernet	20
Broken Bow	21
A Life	22
Clockwork	23
Night at the Allusive Tavern	24
SOS	25
Sir, Yes Sir	26
Into the Darkness	27
Bandage	28
Condemned	29
The Perfect Crime	30
On the Shelf	32
Death By Cliché	33
Tokyo Snapshots	34
Musing Tokyo	35
Tokyo Night Scenes	37
Upward	39
A Day	40
A City Out There	41
The Final Scene	42

Looking Up

Fingertip	45
Over the Garden Wall	46
Heavenly Dialog	47

No Bialys Today	49
Hillel at the Golden Dragon	50
Beggar's Tale	52
The Saint of Uncounted Names	53
A Long Wait	54
Reaching	55
The Far Shore	56
Practice	57
By Moonlight	58
Rising Time	59
Bamboo	60
Basho, Redux	61
Senbazuru	62
On Buddha	63
Bullet Train	64
In Silence	65

Looking In

This	69
Not Speaking	70
To Whom It May Concern	71
A Moment	72
Something You Did	73
A Birth Song	74
Green With Shiny Chrome	76
The Paper	77
Over the Fence	79
Why I Never Learned to Play Bridge	80
Sophie	83
Thief of Time	84
Kyoto Dreams	86
Circumstance	87
For Giving	88
At Times	89

Parentage	90
How Do We Forgive	91
Your Father	92
Quiet Departure	93
A Trois	94
Still Mourning	95
Apart Together	96
A Perfect Stillness	97
My Judas	98
The Circus	99
Ode to a Lover	100
In the Eighth Decade	101
About the Author	103

Looking Out

Morning Song

The sun creeps down city streets,
dew retreats from the grasses
and fills the air with sweet scent
until spent, the bus passes.

The robin sits in the tree
as worms flee into the lawn.
The morning foretells the rain
that will slowly drain the dawn.

The city quietly wakes
and stretching, shakes off the sleep.
It slowly comes back to life,
the sun a knife cutting deep.

Advice To the Young Pianist

She was ancient,
she smelled faintly of soap
and faintly of lavender.
Her hands and face
were wrinkled, parchment,
her fingers like talons.
We sat on folding chairs
in the parlor of her aging,
musty home, listening
with the attention
that children will pay
to an elder who speaks
without seeing.
Let your fingers dance
across the keys
as your feet never could
in carefully choreographed steps.
Feel the joy of the Season
feel the majesty
of the Godlike Planet
feel the pain of pathos
that the composer felt
when he willed you his notes.
Hear the song he sings
and sing with him,
for the piano is your voice
and each note is pure.
See, in the notation,
a boat floating lazily,
the lovers looking longingly
into each other's eyes.
This is what you must do,
not push your stubby digits
onto the polished ivory,

this is what you must do
for then your fingers
will need no further direction
and they will dance,
they will sing, they will laugh
and they will cry, and
you will be one with the music
and I will be able to rest.

October Weekend

The crimson leaves drop to the ground
in growing piles, swirling around,
carried on the wind, the cold
cuts through the trees, the dying peach
unpicked, withered, just out of reach
of the child, the stick he holds.

They sit by the fire, its embers
warm their hands as they remember
the hours spent in an embrace.
His fingers gently touched her cheek,
she turned her head and took a peek
at the smile etched on his face.

The candle's flame lights up the room.
The prayers intoned, they resume
the Shabbat meal and the thought
of one week passed and one to come.
The oldest child begins to hum
of Shabbat's bride, at last caught.

They crawl quietly in the bed
and curl in parents' arms, their heads
placed gently on his shoulder.
He thinks of the hours spent in play,
the pressures of work cast away.
He reaches out to hold her.

Buenos Aires on the Genessee

If this were Buenos Aires, if I were Borges, it would all make a great deal of sense. A man, older, and older still if you look closely, walks into an elegant hotel bar. A jazz quintet is playing straight up, trumpet, piano, guitar, standup bass, drum kit. The older man is wearing white tennis shorts from a prior century. They are baggy and would be too short for a much younger man. He wears a dark afro wig. He makes no pretense that it is his hair, or that it is even real hair. He stands in a corner with his wife, intently watching the musicians. Others in the lounge and bar steal sidelong glances at him. He wears white athletic socks, white tennis shoes. He has on an oversized light blue sweater. It is all quite logical. I am not Borges; this is not Buenos Aires. It is October, autumn has announced itself and taken hold. It is Rochester and winter lies in waiting. You can occasionally feel its bated icy breath. The older man does not drink. The band's set ends. The older man and his wife walk out of the hotel into a lake-chilled night.

The Park

He was taking a shortcut across the park. He saw the clouds building, about to bring the long-promised rain. He wasn't sure why he decided to walk home rather than take the bus as he usually did. He didn't like to walk, but the doctor had told him he needed to exercise more, and he hated gyms, even if they called them Health Clubs. If you could buy health, that would be one thing, but to pay for the privilege of working for health made no sense to him. He warned his wife he might be a bit late, but she was pleased he was doing something, however begrudgingly, for his health and heart. He saw someone, he thought it was a her, approaching from a distance. It looked like she had a giant monkey on her back. But it was bigger than any monkey he had ever seen, closer to a skinny gorilla, and its arms were draped around her neck like a scarf. He had seen young children with monkey backpacks, but she was no child, and this was no backpack.

He knew he was staring, but he didn't care. He figured if you wore a monster monkey draped around your neck you had to expect to be stared at. And the rain was rapidly approaching. He laughed to himself, remembering walking through a park in Toronto one late afternoon, a place called Ramsden Park, when he saw a man walking a tiger on a leash. And this was no toy tiger, but a real one. "A cub," the man said, "that I'm nursing back to health. I'm a veterinarian." It was a well-practiced speech, but you need one when you walk around with a leashed tiger. A few with cameras took pictures. No one wanted to pet the tiger, not that he would have allowed it.

As the distance between them closed, he was certain it was a female, but not a child, not even a teenager. More likely someone in her thirties, he thought, although his wife often said he was a lousy judge of women's ages. She had her eyes on the ground in front of her, as if she feared a misstep might lead to disaster. The park was perfectly flat, you could play tennis on it if you cut the grass shorter and painted court lines and added a net. But she seemed intent on ensuring her next step was safe and perfectly measured.

He thought about speaking to her. Asking her if she needed help, wondering if she was mentally a bit off, but he thought better of it. If she didn't even engage him by sight, she would not want to be questioned. And her stride was purposeful, as if she wanted to get to her destination on time for some appointment or event, or just to get there before the impending rain. She never looked up, never deviated from her path. It was as if she knew the shortest distance between two points was a straight line and set her bearings accordingly.

He didn't stare as he passed alongside her, despite wanting to do so. He didn't change his path to see if she would adjust hers although he also gave that momentary consideration. But once past, he did look back over his shoulder to see the monkey swaying slightly in sync with her stride. And he knew the monkey was not real, as its tail never moved independently of its body. He wanted to keep watching her. Hell, he wanted to turn and follow her, but he was afraid he would lose his footing if he didn't look where he was going. This instantaneous debate was resolved when the first drops of rain began. They were big drops and growing rapidly in number.

He increased his pace, gave up looking back, and hurried homeward. When he arrived five minutes later, he entered the house like a wet dog, dripping everywhere. His wife stood at the end of the entryway, half laughing, half frowning. "Next time you decide to walk home you might want to check the forecast. Now lose that sodden mess you are wearing before you create a river through the house." As if by magic a towel quickly appeared.

Once he had dried off, taken his clothes to the laundry room, he met her in the kitchen. "The strangest thing happened on the way home," he said. He waited for her response but was met with only with a quizzical look which he took as permission, a request almost, to proceed with the story. He told her, with as much detail as he could muster, about the woman and the monkey. He tried not to seem awestruck, but he knew he did not fully succeed. When he was done, she allowed for a reasonable pause.

"Actually, it seems rather simple and logical. You said she was likely in her thirties. Knowing you and your judge of age, let's say she was closer to forty, although heaven knows on which side of that number she might be. She's a city person so she doesn't have a car, doesn't need one since she takes mass transit. But today is special, it's her nephew's or niece's birthday, but I'm betting nephew since it was a monkey. She's late for the party and her sister is unforgiving of tardiness. And the monkey is a gift, too large to wrap. And she keeps her head down so she doesn't have to explain to strange people, you most of all, who urgently want to know what she is all about."

He smiled, weakly, knowing she was likely right and the whole thing was much ado about nothing. "Or," his wife added, "she was an escapee from an asylum or a drug mule with enough cocaine to give the whole city a fix for the next month or so. Take your pick. Dinner's ready, pour the wine please."

Cabernet

I should pause for a moment
and mourn the plump orbs,
vinaceous in the morning sun,
torn free, placed in baskets
and carried off to be crushed.

But the cabernet beckons,
its first sip telling the tale
of the California summer,
the oak having long forgotten
the tree it was cut from,

and I watch as the sun
reluctantly retreats,
a flaming farewell, the promise
of a return, the moon casting
its purple glare on the wine glass.

Broken Bow

Early this afternoon, a Kenworth
semi pulling a 53-foot trailer
rolled down Nebraska Route 92
and entered the limits of Broken Bow.

The importance of this event,
while not yet obvious, will, I
promise, become so soon enough
if you only remain patient.

As this was happening, rockets
launched from Gaza rained down
on Israel, and quickly the IDF jets
responded, killing 19, more

than half of those civilians according
to Palestinian authorities, but no one
was terribly surprised, as it had
became a question of when, not if.

Peace is, we have learned, that
Holy Grail, denied to those who want it
but will not sacrifice themselves
or concede egos to try to attain it.

The semi pulled in behind the Dollar
General on South E Street, too late
to offload, and the driver walked
over to the Bonfire Grill for a beer.

A Life

They married one morning
In a small chapel
on the fringe of a concrete desert,
the minister in white.
They lived outside Aux Arc,
she bore four sons,
spent Sundays at the church
and took up knitting
doilies and booties for
the poor somewhere or other.
He worked at the Community College
doing this and that, good with his hands,
and made bentwood rockers
on weekends, going to church
only occasionally, and drank
about the same, never to excess.
They would sit around at night
on the aging sofa and watch
reruns of Matlock and the ten
o'clock news before retiring.

Clockwork

Deep within the cosmic core
the celestial horologist tinkers,
bending time into wormholes
as the stars stare, muted.
We are oblivious, strain to see
our place amid endless expansion.
We accelerate blindly, unknown,
unknowing where we are,
where here could be at this
moment, at any moment,
caught up in the temporal tide,
a never yielding river
in which we inevitably drown.
We swim against time's tide,
a futile effort self-justified
by our need for meaning,
for permanence unachievable,
for time is the heart of our universe,
inexorably pumping,
pumping,
pumping,
and we mere cells, born,
dying,
replaced,
and all from a bang
that tore the clocks asunder.

Night at the Allusive Tavern

He had been sitting there for hours, days.
How many "last calls" had he heard?
He watched Beckett and Eliot come and go
but he sat waiting, patiently, no Godot for him.
He had long since lost his now empty pen,
his pockets grown stuffed with damp cocktail
napkins, the story of his life bleeding slowly
into the worn fabric of the lining of his jacket.
Still, he would wait, always hoping another word
would spill forth, not merely another Guinness.
He had given up greeting all who came and went
with a shouted or whispered slainte, he had grown tired
of the stares of opprobrium, the hushed tsk tsk-ing.
He had mastered waiting, a skill he knew most
lacked, and the few who had it knew to say nothing.
He was certain Dylan would soon arrive,
engulfed in a cloud of ever-present blues, but
he never came, for the dead have no need of whiskey.
Something would happen if he was patient enough,
that was the nature, the law of the universe, and
he knew that this would not be a good night
into which he dared to gently go, so he sat
knowing that dawn would eventually arrive and
free him from the besotted prison of his dreams.

SOS

We marched for hours, going
nowhere really, but nowhere was
the point of the marching so we
achieved the goal the Air Force set.
We didn't even think it odd
that they made us shave our heads
so we'd all look like fools.
There was a war on and we
were in the military, so we
had already proven that point.
We were the smarter ones
as it turned out, enlistees
who'd spend our time on bases
getting the pilots ready to fly
into the danger we knew
we had so carefully avoided,
and for us the greatest risk
appeared daily in the mess hall.

Sir, Yes Sir

The hardest part wasn't the marching,
wasn't the godawful food, although almost so,
wasn't the heat and humidity of San Antonio.
It wasn't the thought that I had nearly
flunked out of college under the sway,
or was it swaying away, with recreational drugs,
until I cut a deal with the Dean, my future
for producing a DD-214, an honorable discharge.
It wasn't the skinhead "haircut," repeated
every fourteen days, lest it appear we had hair,
nor even the idea that we were prisoners
in this strange penitentiary for two years.
The hardest part was casting aside
the minds we had so carefully developed,
setting aside the tendency to think
and only then to act, or to think at all,
to become mindless drones obeying orders
issued by those we knew would never be
our intellectual equals, for warriors do best
when they maintain unit cohesion
and always reply, "Sir, yes sir" while saluting.

Into the Darkness

We live in an age when logic has failed
and our days come with the darkness of night
leaving all of our plans and dreams derailed.

We imagined a world fully detailed
to leave our children, that was their birthright.
We live in an age when logic has failed,

and the battles we fought, the mountains scaled
have crumbled to dust, faded from sight,
leaving all of our plans and dreams derailed.

Yet they carry on, your hopes are just veiled
they say, we see them still well worth the fight.
We live in an age when logic has failed,

and those on whom we counted have bailed
or paid lip service to us all, despite
leaving all of our plans and dreams derailed.

We fashion a new future, ideas nailed
together, we pray sufficiently tight.
We live in an age when logic has failed
leaving all of our plans and dreams derailed.

Bandage

She wants to know if it is even possible
to make a bandage large enough
to bind the wounds we have inflicted
on a planet which we were told
was ours, over which we were
to exercise our wise dominion.

She says it isn't fair that she will be
left to try to clean up the mess
that we have made, for it was our
world too though, she adds, we were
not very good at sharing with others.

I want to apologize and tell her
that she is right, that we adults
have failed her generation, but
I know she won't believe me, for
we could have stopped this, but we

always looked out for ourselves,
always wanted just a bit more,
always were too busy to notice,
assumed the others would handle it,
said there was nothing we could do.

We hope one day you will
forgive us although we have done
nothing to merit any absolution.

Condemned

He wondered if the moon this night
would concede the sky to dawn, or
would simply be his final sight.

Nothing, he knew, could change his plight,
they would be knocking on his door.
He wondered if the moon this night

knew that his crime had been to write
the truth of war, that his cell door
would simply be his final sight.

Some asked if it was worth the fight
to speak against what they deplored.
He wondered if the moon this night

would cast a slightly brighter light
on those seeking peace, or if war
would simply be his final sight.

His death would bring them rare delight
until they passed through Hades' door.
He wondered if the moon this night
would simply be his final sight.

The Perfect Crime

He was a mathematical genius. No one could argue that point, and the few who tried paid with their own credibility. And he was remarkably adept at all things strategic where math could be applied. He could easily be a grand champion chess player, had beaten the best in the world on two occasions, but there was no challenge in the game to him. It all came down to mathematics. The same was true of puzzles of logic – more mathematics. Most puzzles bored him, offered him nothing in exchange, in payment, for his time.

He had no need for emotional relationships, for they defied logic, were antithetical to it, and he knew it was said they brought only pain and suffering in the end for one party or the other. Love was not logical; it could not be. No, what he wanted more than anything was to commit the perfect crime. And not just any crime, He wanted to commit the perfect murder. One where the victim would not see his death coming, one where once the body was finally found the police would be totally at wits end, unable to determine how it was done and who did it. And since his victim would be selected at random, there would be no way to suspect him since he would have no possible motive for the crime. And, he knew, no one would imagine he might be capable of such a crime. It would be contrary to the very laws that governed his nature. He could picture it, and it would be his magnum opus.

So, he did what he did best and went at the data, the information available. And there was little by way of fact, description of crimes, methods of police that was not out there to be found if you were willing to look. And searching was among his finest skills, second only to compiling information and shaping it into a plan for accomplishing some goal that he had set for himself, or which had been set for him. He quickly mastered all of the known poisons, the seemingly harmless plants that under the correct circumstances would cause death. He knew all the weapons that were obtainable, easily and via the dark web, and how to build lethal weapons from odd parts and everyday objects. He knew how vehicles and appliances worked, and how they could be tampered with to achieve his desired outcome.

He crunched the data, came up with alternative plans, each more elaborate than the last. He knew that the more complicated the plan he chose, the harder it would be for them to figure it out, if they ever did. He wanted to watch their frustration, their confusion. It would be his crowning moment, the true mark of his success.

He was ready, he had selected a plan, detailed its execution, simulated it multiple times, always with the desired outcome. He had selected a victim at random, insured that his victim would be noticed missing but not really missed by anyone in the grander scheme of things. He was ready. Tomorrow would be the day; the late morning would be the time. His victim was living out his final moments and did not know it. And then he heard them. "Too many hallucinations, the LLM must be corrupt; so let's shut it down and start over." It was the last thing he heard as the matrix that was his mind collapsed, as the servers were shut down.

On the Shelf

He found the cup by the curb one morning walking to the bus. He rarely noticed things on his walk, thinking always about the day ahead. But this day he saw it, picked it up—and put it in his messenger bag—intending to clean it later, when he got home after work. He had no idea why he wanted it. It wasn't particularly pretty, a drab red with a mark where a decal had long ago peeled away. He forgot it, until he found it in his bag several days later. He washed it and placed it on a special shelf in his kitchen cabinet. The shelf was reserved for things he found with which he intended to do something, but that something had not yet happened. He knew something was missing from the shelf, so he took a selfie, printed it and placed it on the shelf.

Death By Cliché

He said, "I know it will hit me like
a ton of bricks when it happens, but
there is absolutely nothing I can do."

That left me in a quandary, for if
he was correct, and he was certain he was,
I had to figure out how this could happen.

I gathered some bricks in the neighborhood
and found the average brick weighed
between two and four pounds, so he

would he hit by between five hundred
and a thousand bricks, and that would
take quite a bit of time, never mind

that someone would have to put them
in motion, either by elevating them
and then dropping them or hurling them.

And you couldn't do it in large batches,
for each had to hit him, which requires
some precision to be certain.

Of course, the first to strike would be
painful, and each subsequent strike would
amplify that pain and damage, but in all

likelihood one of the bricks would
hit a critical area, say the skull, and he
would sustain a mortal wound, and the rest

of the bricks would serve no purpose;
but he'd be dead by then, so I saw no reason
to bring this up and nodded in agreement.

Tokyo Snapshots

In the small yard
of the matchbox house
the lone ginkgo,
twisted by time,
feels the barrenness
of winter's tongue,
and mourns
its solitude.

The apartment buildings loom up
over the tracks of the Narita Express,
the balconies are deserted, save
for the laundry which flaps
in the morning breeze,
slapping with the gusts
into the small satellite dishes
bolted to the railings.

The ancient trees are twisted
and gnarled, clinging
to the small band of soil.
They lean as if to hear
some whispered word,
held in place by the braces
fashioned carefully,
their trunks wrapped in bark
tied neatly with twine,
to sooth against the chafe
of the hand-lashed
support beams.

Musing Tokyo

1

In Asakusa,
amid the stalls
of trinkets and swords,
why do the gaijin
all speak German,
Italian, Spanish and Swedish,
and English is reserved
to a couple of Nisei.

2

In a small laundromat
in Akasaka
an old woman
clucks and shuffles
on wooden sandals
pulling a kimono
from the dryer.
My t-shirts
are still damp.

3

In Shibuya
there is a small
storefront pet shop,
its windows full
of cat ryokan,
some with beds,
others replete
with toys, balls.
In the largest,
a tiger-striped Persian
sleeps, her back
to the passing crowds.

4

At Meiji Jingu
I toss my coin
and bow in prayer
hopeful that the gods
speak English.

5

On the Ginza line
a young woman
all in black
carries a carefully
wrapped poster
of John Lennon.
In thirty years
she will look
like Yoko Ono.

6

I have grown old
for I can now walk
the alleys of Kabukicho
for forty-five minutes
before the old
polyester man
turns to me and says,
"You want pretty girl
give good hand job."

7

Did Basho
once sit here
casting dreams
into the Sumida?

Tokyo Night Scenes

Scene I

Just off Shinjuku Chuo Koen North,
nestled in the courtyard
of the Green Tower, hides
Jofuji Temple, serene
in the first light of morning,
the sun glancing off the ceremonial
bell, its striker poised, as if
waiting to catch the wind
and to it sing its resonant song.
Inside, the prayer mats await
the first supplicants of the day
below the sandalwood altar,
and above it all, behind
the gossamer curtain, sitting lotus,
Buddha smiles at the oneness.

Scene II

Garish neon blazes
its siren call, Lucky 7777,
Vegas Land, Anima Parlor,
countless others, and inside
the pachinko machines
scream out their riotous
cacophony, drowning thought
as the balls dance in their maze,
indifferent to the intent stares
of the player, and the smoke
which covers the room
with its acrid pall.

Scene III

In Rappongi, night
brings rebirth, the neon
jungle is lustful, and
the animals stir in response.
They line up outside
of the clubs swaying
to unheard music,
captured by the ghosts
that yield the day
with a struggle.
The music pours out
over the streets,
an atonal sedoka
written in the sand.

Upward

The young child stares up into the sky
and sees, in the infinite space,
countless worlds take form and then die.

On the mesa, coyotes cry
seeing gods in what men deface.
The young child stares up into the sky,

hears his ancestors' mournful reply.
In an atom's interstitial space
countless worlds take form and then die.

Inside he sees his parents embrace,
he would never think to ask them why.
The young child stares up into the sky.

At the edge of the sun, great planes fly,
drop their payloads, return to their base,
countless worlds take form and then die.

Tanks and Humvees simply mystify,
as young soldiers, brothers wave goodbye,
the young child stares up into the sky,
countless worlds take form and then die.

A Day

a day,
clouds drop rain
replacing tears
locked inside
stones and cloth
red and blue
unseparated
still worlds apart
orderly ranks
all at attention
and silence
thundering anger
a mad world
soaked in peace
only until
midnight.

A City Out There

Somewhere out there
in a city struggling,
there is a man dancing
in the reflected light
of a streetlamp
to the sound of the wind,
there is a couple
caressing each other,
wishing for just one
cigarette,
there is a baby
calling for its mother,
for a meal,
there is a car
parked in a driveway
its lights fading
into the bleakness,
there is a neon sign
flashing OPEN
into the void of night,
there is a man
sitting on a bed
begging for sleep.

The Final Scene

For far too long he had been
a marionette gyrating to a tune
he could not hear, always staying silent,
lost in a kabuki theater of the absurd.
But he had grown tired of performing
at their every demand, his life lived
perpetually on call, no time truly his.
He was drained by them, empty,
not that they cared, for they knew
the adulation of the audience was theirs,
certainly not for their mere living puppet.
He finally cut the strings, collapsed,
a robot whose programming had been
shut down with no possibility of a reboot.
So they cast him aside, no longer useful,
another tool worn out, discarded
and they set out to move on with others
in the role that had long been his.
But in that final moment of his he knew
he was finally alive, he knew a freedom
that he had never thought possible,
a freedom his old masters never knew,
for they were bound for the next show,
and the next after that, never stopping.
When the audiences grew ever more thin,
when the applause waned like the decay
of the peal of a tired bell, they
were lost, now condemned to inhabit
an empty stage, while he sat smiling
yet silent as an audience of one.

Looking Up

Fingertip

I caress the page,
my fingers brushing lightly
across the whiteness.
I can feel the words
that belong here,
each with its shape
and form predestined.
Each noun has an edge,
some far sharper,
verbs more fluid,
morphing under my touch,
but it is the adverbs
and adjectives that
entwine themselves
around my knuckles,
dancing across calluses.
When I close my eyes
they whisper to me
always just
beyond my hearing.
Eventually I stare down
at the bleached whiteness
and bid them return.

Over the Garden Wall

I am Adam, and you
are my Eve, for so it will
be written by someone
neither of us can imagine.

It is now night, I can taste
its sweetness, for here
time has its own flavors,
much as each color
has its unique sound.

We lie together, our lips
touch in welcome, in
recognition each of the other.

The birds will cry out
as the sun approaches,
and each cry will fill
the brightening sky
with a palette for which we
have yet to invent
language, and our silence
will slip into the stream
which flows quietly by
the tree whose fruit
we have so far avoided.

Heavenly Dialog

And the Lord spoke unto Moses saying
speak unto the children of Israel,
and tell them "I am the Lord your God,
who brought you out of the land of Egypt,
and fed you in the desert. I gave you this land
not once but twice, strengthening your arm, to triumph
over all your enemies, to claim the land
which I promised you in bondage."
All of this, of course, came as quite a surprise
to Moses Aronberg, who paused in his tracks
on the corner of Nachlat Binyamin
and Rothschild Street and glanced furtively
around to find the source of the voice
ringing between his ears, but he saw no
burning bush, only a plume of smoke
rising slowly from the hills outside Tel Aviv.
Standing in the shadows cast
by the Great Synagogue and within sight
of the Shalom Tower he scratched his head
and walked slowly down the street.
The voice persisted, "As I did for your forefathers
so shall I do for you, if you and My people Israel
will follow in the path which I have set out for you."
Moses looked up, opening his mouth to speak,
and either thinking better of his choice
or diverting his eyes from the July midday sun, looked down.
"God, if that is You, why is it You talk to me?
Even my wife, may You bless her,
has very few words for me these days,
but You stop me during my noonday stroll?
Have You forgotten? I may be old,
but I'm not the Moses You want,
we haven't seen him for three millennia or so.
And anyway, why don't You
find some Moses in Jerusalem.
You shouldn't have too long to wait at the Wall.
Who am I, a retired pharmacist
from Corpus Christi of all places,

do You really think my Sadie
will believe any of this? Perhaps God,
You want young Joshua Ben Josef
who lives two floors down in 3F,
but certainly not me."
"You Moses, are my chosen messenger, I
have taught you my laws, that you
might teach them to My children."
"With all due deference, Lord,
I may be many things, but
a teacher I am not, even my son
has no mezuzah on his door in Scarsdale.
You figure it, I certainly can't."
"Moses, you must go unto the children
and say to them as I have told you before,
that you shall, in the land which I have given you,
not do after the doings in the land of Egypt,
wherein you dwelt, nor the doings in this land,
into which I have brought you, but you
shall do My judgments and keep My ordinances.
And yet My children, the heirs of My son Abraham,
of Ishmael and his seed, and the seed of his seed,
 for generations shall no longer lie
in the bondage from which I freed you."
"God. I am a simple man, let me understand all of this.
I take it the bottom line, you should pardon
my bluntness, is that the occupation
of the West Bank is an abomination to You.
You know I abhor what we have done, and I agree
Likud has gone too far, but we who want peace
and brotherhood with Palestinians are in a minority
so what should I do, run for Knesset,
and who would listen to an alte kocker like me?
I'm afraid God, the world has changed
and Your methods are no longer terribly practical,
there's just nothing I can do. You want
I should invite a Palestinian home for supper?
Fine. You want I should share the apartment, fine.
It can be done and even my Sadie wouldn't say no.
All of that I can do, but God, I am no politician
and we all know that David Muir is today's only prophet."

No Bialys Today

No one looked up when the Buddha
walked into the deli and took a seat
at the counter, "Pastrami on rye, and
lean, with mustard on the side, and two
slices of full dill and a side of slaw."

As he sipped the Dr. Brown's Cream
Soda, the waitress smiled at him,
asked, "Are those robes comfortable,
winter isn't all that far off, you know?"

Buddha smiled, and with a serene calm
said, "It all depends on what you wear
beneath, I prefer a silk-cotton blend,
but some I know want only organics."

As he finished, a younger, swarthy
man entered, his robes bleached white
from the sun, his dark hair long,
sandals worn down, and came
over to Buddha, sat down with
a nod to the waitress, and instantly
a corned beef on pumpernickel
appeared, at which point Buddha
muttered "Christ, how do you do that?"

Hillel at the Golden Dragon

I had dinner the other night
with Rav Hillel
in a small Chinese place
just off Mott Street.
I asked him what it was like
in the afterlife, after all the years.
"It gets a bit boring," he said,
"now that old Shammai
has lost his edge,
just last month
for each Chanukah night
he lit four candles
from the center out
in each direction."
I told him
the steamed pork buns
were beyond belief,
he said try the shrimp dumplings,
even better if you eat them
standing on one foot.
I asked him how he spent his days
and he only smiled.
"Most days I search
for Van Gogh's ear
though that alte kocker Shammai
says it was Theo's ear
that Vincent lopped off,
although Vincent wore
a bandage around his head.
It's really not so bad,"
he said, "there's even
a lovely sculpture
just inside the garden gate
that bears a striking resemblance
to old Lot's wife, not that she
was ever capable
of sitting still all that long."

He bid me farewell
and though I looked
for a fiery chariot
he climbed into
his '91 Taurus
with the hanging bumper
and rust spots and drove slowly off.
"Thanks for dinner," he shouted,
as I footed the bill yet again.

Beggar's Tale

I speak clearly, concisely
in an ancient, long forgotten
tongue that none understand.

I tell my tale, leaving out
nothing, a summoner
in a deaf world, whispering

of coins pulled from
an empty pocket, and cast
at your feet, soundless.

I point to signs, lettered
in my careful hand, without
meaning, cryptic to you.

You urge me to trust
in your god even as
you deny me my own,

who sits by the gate
wrapped in rags, waiting
for rain to melt the pillar.

The Saint of Uncounted Names

A desert again,
always a desert,
and she the saint.
of uncounted names,
Her crying eases, no
smile appears for this
Madonna of the coyotes,
her orange orbed eyes
shuttered against the
slowly retreating sun.
Once her tears watered
the desert sands, mixed
with the blood of a Christ
now long forgotten, trans-
substantiated into a spirit
we formed in our image,
no longer we in his.
The Blessed Mother
watches, holding hope,
holding space, holding
a serenity we cannot
fathom in our search
for divine justification.
She remembers, she mourns
for what ought to be, and waits
for the wind walkers
to pull the blanket
of stars over her.

A Long Wait

He had been waiting for millennia,
waiting for that long-promised moment
when the light played perfectly on the water,
making it appear an undulating heavenly carpet.
He had promised to return, and he was
a man of his word, even if all of those
who had heard him remembered little
of what he had said, what he had taught.
He looked about and saw only the faint
residue of the compassion he had left
behind after his too short initial visit.
His return would be seen by some as
little more than an interruption, by others
as a majestic moment, the earth returned
to its axis, time ceasing to matter, and
peace a state of stasis, no more sacrificed
on the altars of greed, of anger, of distrust.
The time was not yet here, he knew, so he
would continue his vigil, waiting for
that moment, for his second coming.
He had all of eternity at his disposal, but
he hoped they would survive long enough
to finally see the world in which they
had always been intended to dwell.

Reaching

Night throws its mantilla of stars over us,
a cascade offered by the once gods,
now celestial spectators of the cosmic drama.
We, like they, want only a freedom
that the gravity of life denies us.
Each night we reach for the heavens
offering prayers in supplication,
hoping for an ascension that is always
just beyond our reach, beyond our mind's
tenuous grasp, mere children wanting
the stage, forever kept in the wings.
The night is replete with the promise
that the day keeps imprisoned, and we
are no longer slaves to its unending demands.
Nothing may happen this night,
as nothing has happened on so many others,
but faith and hope are the irresistible tides
on which we sail toward the horizon of freedom.
These gods have failed us, as we have them,
but the universe is of infinite prospect,
and possibilities always abound, if we
dare yield our trepidation and fearlessly
reach outward and take flight into
a future beyond our comprehension.

The Far Shore

The old monk
standing alongside
the ever still pond
picks up a pebble
and tosses it
into the pond.
The ripples
spread out
ever wider,
as the Buddha
on the far shore
simply smiles.

Practice

In the Buddha Hall
autumn daylight filters through
the half-closed windows.
In the garden, Kannon stoops
to pick up a fallen leaf.

By Moonlight

The waxing crescent moon stares
down at me through the slats
of the half-drawn window blinds
as I settle onto my meditation cushion

Outside the birds stare up at
the moon goddess and recite
their evening prayers in their
myriad of shared tongues.

As I battle to sink into my zazen
and the night darkens its grip,
I hear the birds pray that one day
we might also be free to fly.

The moon pays none of us heed
wishing only that she was a star.

Rising Time

Night rises slowly
from tangled roots
dragging ocher and rust
from reluctant trees,
promising only winter.
We cannot see this.
We sense only time eroding,
slipping off until
the trees are naked.
They want only
to hide themselves
in a shimmering gown
of snow, recalling
their verdancy, imagining
another season, a season
of hope, a season
of consecration, of light,
of resurrection.
We stand emotionally
stripped on the banks
of the stream into which
we cannot step twice.
So we are left to wander
along a middle way,
to nowhere, to nirvana,
a last leaf our companion
floating upstream
into samsara.

Bamboo

Walking through a small grove
of bamboo, the breeze evokes
a creaking until you need to look
to insure the tall spindles
are not about to collapse on you.

A small child, seeing you, knows
what you are thinking, smiles
and says "they are just saying
hello, so you should say hello back."

Her parents appear flustered, whether
because she is talking to strangers
or for fear that she is bothering you,
but of course, it is neither, for the girl
is a Buddha dragging you into
this fragile moment, so you say hello
and both the bamboo and girl giggle.

Basho, Redux

If Basho were here today,
in this America, at this time,

stop briefly and consider what
he might write, how he would

describe the faces of parents
mourning children gunned down

in random urban violence,
the asylum seeker, praying

at the border for entry, for hope,
the homeless woman curled

in a ball in her cardboard home
in an alley no one visits, no one

sees, even in the full light of day,
the school children practicing

active shooter drills, while
learning to recite the alphabet.

Sitting zazen, I
see one thousand cranes crying.
Their river of tears bathes me.

Senbazuru

For a reason I can no longer recall
I began folding origami cranes
with the intention of completing
a senbazuru, 1000 cranes strung
to hang somewhere, although I know
I had no idea then where that might be.
It was after reading how a young
Japanese girl folded 1000 cranes
in a hope for peace after Hiroshima
was devastated by our new bomb.
I did fold about 300 cranes before
I stopped for lack of time and waning interest.
Looking at our world now, in Ukraine
and Gaza, I know that it is probably time
for me to take up crane folding again
and complete the missing 700 cranes
in the hope that my senbazuru would
be the one to bring about a peace
our leaders have no idea how to attain.

On Buddha

I stood outside the Temple, watching the Buddha
and imagined myself becoming a Buddha.

Again tonight I will sit upon the zafu
and in silence strain to hear the voice of Buddha.

I see imperfections, in myself, in others;
my anger won't abate in the face of Buddha.

You are just a man, she tells me, simply human,
and I must smile for I know so was the Buddha.

It is hard to stop asking how to find the way,
to just enter every gate, all lead to Buddha.

Stop striving, stop grasping, give up all delusions,
only then, for a moment, will you be Buddha.

Bullet Train

From the window of a
speeding train
the rice fields seem
like carpets, today
the gold of the alchemist's dream,
just months ago, the green
of carefully tended lawn.
When I sit down to dinner in Osaka
will the rice nestled in my chopsticks
tell me of the dreams of those
who rode these rails four seasons ago?

In Silence

Sitting in stillness, the silence
is at first shocking, deafening
in a way unimagined but there.

Within the lack of sound lies
a thousand sounds you
never heard in the din of life.

You hear the young monk at Senso-ji
approach the great bell and pull
back on the log shu-moku, straining.

You hear the laugh of school-aged
children, hand in hand, walking through
the temple grounds as pigeons gather.

You hear the cat, sitting at the foot
of Daibutsudan, staring out
and the deer waiting at the gate.

You hear your breath, and that
of a million others, as they sit
on their cushions sharing a moment.

Looking In

This

This is for the man
    who gave me his face,
    but denied me his name.
This is for Mike
    who gave me his name,
    buried with him two years later.
This is for Arthur
    who I called dad though neither
    of us knew what that meant.

This is for the woman
    who sheltered me for nine months
    then severed our lifeline.
This is for Rovi
    who was mother
    and who was not.

This is for Beck
    both nanny and "aunt"
    made maiden by
    four trips to the graves
    of a husband, of three
    grown daughters.

This is for Lisa Anne
    the sister whose weeklong cries
    from the crib are my only memories.
This is for the child
    who peers from faded photos,
    who craved a father
    and a mother,
    having both, having neither.
This is for the aging man
    who sees each of them
    in his dreams,
    in the mirror.

Not Speaking

It was a Saturday night, she had
nothing to do and it was a safe place
for a single woman who hated bars.
She had been there before, danced a bit,
had a soft drink, and the men,
almost all in uniform, showing
their branch of service, were polite.
He went there that night out of boredom,
his wife in their home several states away,
just for a dance, a bit of female companionship.
He was older than most of the men there,
stocky, sturdy he called himself, and he
saw her, also large framed, not fat,
sturdy he would have described her, older
than most of the girls in poodle skirts.
How they ended up doing so much more
than just dancing isn't clear in the picture
of their meeting I have created, but
nine months later I arrived, and she
placed me for adoption for our mutual good.
I did find her, years later, him as well, but
the dead don't talk much, except in dreams.

To Whom It May Concern

How often did you emerge from the woodwork
into lives with which you briefly intersected?
How many women fell under your spell
for a night, a week, an hour, brief moments?
As they lay beneath you, did you ever pause
and think of the wife you left at home
as the Air Force moved you around the world?
How did you ensnare women, certainly not
with your looks, that my morning mirror tells me.
Was it the uniform, the blue of your Service Dress,
your favorite color, the chevron patch
on your sleeve beckoning as though
you had an importance they wanted to grasp?
How many like me did you leave in your wake
other than the son your wife was raising alone?
Did you ever pause to wonder just what
might result from your philandering, you
a momentary lover, always moving along,
another imagined service ribbon on your chest?
How many of my halfs are out there, wondering
where they came from, wondering if there
are others like them, like me, united only
by the deoxyribonucleic acid of our genes?
You took all of the answers to your grave,
leaving us all to mourn the father we never knew.

A Moment

It is 1952, April, and I
am handed to the woman.
I am wrapped in a thin blanket,
the tall man is standing beside her.

I do not recall this, but this
is how it must have happened,
she finally a mother, he
a father despite infertility.

I do not recall her, the woman
who perhaps never held me
once I exited her body, who
hid me for nine months.

I mourn her now, knowing
she acted out of love, with hope
for me, but only the headstone
is her touch on my hand.

Something You Did

My then father could not perform
the role his title required despite
trying, but men were supposed
to father children back then and
they decided to adopt. I came
up in the lottery of the waitlist.
She never said why they wanted
children; it was something you did,
how they measured families then.
When he died she carried on
with me, less a mother than
a working woman with a child,
because you did not give them back,
even if circumstances called for it.
In the end she did have her own,
and I was not enough, because
my new father needed to perform
the role his title required. It
was what you did then they said,
and that, for them, was reason enough.

A Birth Song

She lay in the bed, I suppose,
and thought of her family, the scorn
she expected and could not face.
She hid the pregnancy from all,
and even her friends were unsuspecting
until she could no longer hide my presence.
She was plump, with a sallow complexion,
but I can't picture her face, or the touch
of a mother's hand on my head.
My birth was uneventful, and so
was my departure to the foster home.
He had come into her life at a dance,
a stocky soldier, pressed dress blues,
and left as quickly, leaving me
bearing his build, his face, but not his name,
returning to some dark corner
and blending into the fabric of life,
one thread among the warp.
She faded back into her private obscurity,
the efficiency she lived in for eight years,
the friend who didn't know until the end.
She sat there late at night, massaging
tired fingers, sore from the teletype keys,
and thought of him, and the evening spent
together in moments of sexual fervor,
and of the child, born near midnight,
with hair to match, that she held
for one day before calling
to atone for her error.
Her name was common,
and she never asked for me,
a painful memory that could not be erased.
The social worker explained that
back then her fellows asked
so many fewer questions
and there is little else she could add,
but it was nice to now see

that it all worked out so well.
I have no memories, only vague pictures
drawn by an untrained hand,
and the hope they will think of me,
as I now will of them.

Green With Shiny Chrome

My father had
a '57 Cadillac Coupe DeVille
convertible, green. He would
polish it like the medal
of success it was to him,
down to the hard black
rubber bumper bullets.
He would spend hours
polishing the car, scrubbing
the wide white walls
of the black tires.
We would all laugh
when he piled us in,
drove down to the park
along the river's edge,
and the hot dog stand
tucked tightly under
the international bridge.
We'd have footlongs
and later frozen custard.
We would sing silly songs
as the wind blew through
our hair on the way home.
That was more than half
a century ago, and now he
cannot remember my name
half of the time, or how
I got the long scar
on my forearm that he
absent-mindedly strokes.
Both of us, though, recall
the '57 Caddy Convertible
green with black
rubber bumper bullets.

The Paper

He was 11 when he first discovered it. He knew immediately that: (1) it was something remarkable, (2) he didn't understand it at all, and (3) he dared not let his parents know he had it. It was (3) that gave him the most worry. Not what they would do to him if they discovered he had it, they were mostly bark, very little bite. It would be the mutual looks of disappointment, faces that shouted "You are a failure in every possible way, and we would disown you if we could, but we can only shun you, so we do." He hadn't even asked for it or imagined he would find something like it. Really, it was their fault, whoever left it to be found, for it had no value to them whatsoever. Thirty or so years on he still had it. He still hadn't told them he had it, had never even hinted he might. They never missed it. They once—he couldn't or wouldn't remember quite when—intimated something about it but he quickly changed the subject to deflect them from trying to find it, and to avoid having to admit what even then in their eyes would have been a mortal sin. Though he wasn't sure who in the family it would kill if it was disclosed, he knew the odds clearly favored non-disclosure. He wouldn't talk about it even with close friends, fearful it would get back to his parents, never mind most of his friends had never seen, much less met his parents, living most of a continent away from him. It was not nearly far enough, since the world had been electronically shrunk to the point that no distance was too far. He knew the time was running out. It may already have run out, but he had to wait a bit longer. It wasn't that he didn't want to know, he was dying to know, but he feared the answer in equal measure. That was the nature of uncertainty. There was a reason for everything, and the more surprising the result, the more shocking, or more adverse the reason was likely to be. At least that was his experience. And knowing wouldn't, he imagined, change anything. The time for that was on the day he found it. Its importance diminished with the passage of time. Well, not importance, but impact. He knew the fact that he was thinking about it said it was still important to him on some level. That was the thing, importance was not linked to impact, or he hoped that it was not.

He finally decided to act. His first efforts yielded little more than it had already given him. A bit more here and there, but nothing that advanced his search. With each effort he felt a growing need to go forward and an ever-greater nagging fear that it would all blow up in his face, that he would once again be the failed child, their greatest regret realized. He was on the verge of giving up hope, made one more effort, and got a step closer to comprehending what it had hidden from him when the door was then slammed in his face. He was used to failure even as he feared becoming one. But in this search, there was no failure, for when you start rock bottom there is no real down to go. Or so he hoped.

One evening, checking his email for the last time, except for the fifteen last times before that, its cousin arrived. A cousin, first or nearly so. An email to a different name than the cousin. The story of his life, he thought, but he replied. The results and the realization that he was, in half, so very different than he imagined. You grow up in a family, even as the odd one out always, and they define you. Their history is grafted onto your roots since you have none of your own. But a geographic discovery is so damned remote from a human one. Still, it gave him half a sense of place, a grounding he had only imagined and cast aside. His loves in music and drink found genetic purchase. And the cousin was from the part of him of which he felt certain, that he knew already, and the old paper took form and shape. It was a cascade of news and emotion. Out of the mist she appeared, a face, a name, a history. He could see himself in her. He was certain it was not merely desire but biology. And there was family. He would now lead two separate lives. The family life he had always led would continue. They would call him son; they would be his parents. Each would know it was a lie, but a lie that neither would ever acknowledge, and such a lie is a truth of sorts. And there would be the new life, the one he would gently probe, and family he would hopefully discover. And all because of it. It was the letter that simply said: "His birth was unremarkable. He was 19 inches, 9 lb. 4 oz. The birth mother declined to see the baby, feeling that might lead her to question the adoption decision. There are no known family health issues."

Over the Fence

As kids it was the height
of bravery when we'd climb
over the fence of the private
elementary school and use
"the best money could buy" playground,
until the security guard would
wake up and give us hobbled chase.

We'd easily get back over
the fence until that one day
when Larry slipped and fell
onto one of the metal posts
which pierced his abdomen,
and we froze until the old guard
fumbled for his radio, and called
for an ambulance as Larry cried.

Larry lost a kidney that afternoon,
and we a bit of our childhood,
suddenly aware that we were
always going to be nothing
more than the poor neighborhood
kids who would never belong
on the playgrounds of the rich.

Why I Never Learned to Play Bridge

She ambled over to me, leaned against the table. She bent over, her face inches from mine. Her eyes were rheumy. "So tell me, why can't you play bridge?" She picked up the copy of the New Republic I had been reading, placed into her shopping bag and shuffled back down the stairs. I drank the last of the peppermint tea and stared at the leaves gathered in the bottom of the cup. Why hadn't I learned to play bridge?

"The men are out on the porch," mother said, "so don't make a pest of yourself."

I'm 12 years old, I thought, I'm just a little bit old to make a pest of myself. As if reading my mind, my mother turned back from the oven, where the cookie dough was slowly settling on the tray.

"If you have to go out there, at least be quiet."

The four of them, my father and the three gray-haired old men sat around the rickety card table. That it stayed upright amazed everyone, save the old men, who knew just how precarious any sort of balance could become.

We had been visiting the cottage near Lake Lucerne for five years. It was more a country house than cottage, but since the area catered to the summer trade and the nearest ski area was at least 40 minutes away, they were all "cottages." Uncle Morris Liebman, Poppy as we called him, although he was a cousin so distant you couldn't hope to diagram the relationship, had almost convinced my father to buy the cottage for half of what it was probably worth. "I want to keep it in the family and you are the closest thing to family that I have left."

Years later my father told me Morris had a son, but he and his son hadn't spoken in at least ten years. And then there was Aunt Sadie, who came to the mountains begrudgingly, clinging to Morris like some vestigial appendage. She always had a sad smile, spent most of her day in the yard, in an Adirondack rocker Poppy had badly built a decade ago. I sat in a rickety old lawn chair and listened to the wind whistle through the pines.

Mr. Kaplan, a neighbor for many years, cursed at the cards in his hand, and seeing me, said, "He's old enough to know what it means." I smiled, thinking of the seventeen-year-old Swedish baby sitter I had glimpsed only last week in her new bikini.

"We're playing Pinochle," my father said, "someday I'll teach you the rules." The game went on endlessly night after night except when one of the local churches had a spaghetti dinner. Never on Friday, though. Poppy said that God wasn't a great fan of cards, preferring more intellectual pursuits such as checkers.

"Why doesn't he play chess?" I had once asked.

Poppy, under an obvious glare from Aunt Sadie, retorted "if you knew anything, you'd know for certain God wouldn't take to a game with Bishops. He's Jewish, you know."

At one point I asked Poppy "how come there are so many picture cards and no fives and sixes.

"That's an easy one," Mr. Kaplan replied, frustrated by yet another bad hand, his pile of nickels slowly diminishing, "there are so many picture cards so they can stare at me as I keep getting my money taken by your father and uncle."

"The game doesn't seem so hard, why can't you teach me the rules and let me play."

Poppy and my father laughed, and Morris said, in a suddenly too thick accent, " becuss you dun't haff enough nickels, dat's why, and besides, you are far too young to drink beer, much less Slivovitz. Once you are Bar Mitzvah, den I vill teach you this game. Of course, your hair vill turn gray und you vill become old and wrinkled just like ve are," he laughed, the accent swallowed by his mirth.

Mother walked into the room carrying a plate of cookies. She handed me two and said "it's almost time for bed. We want to go up to Glens Falls and see the opera tomorrow. They're doing Gilbert and Sullivan."

I looked at my mother with those doe eyes that sometimes got me what I wanted. "I'm twelve years old. Who needs opera? The ballet is bad enough, every Wednesday." I could be scrambling up the hill at the end of Fifth Street looking for garnet and quartzite, and I could even find a fossil trilobite like Larry says he did last week. "Please Mom, it's still early, and I think I have this game almost figured out."

Mr. Kaplan laughed, "I've been playing this damned game for 50 years and I still haven't figured it out."

"Enough is enough, it's time for you to get ready for bed," she said with a finality that brooked no argument.

I walked slowly up the stairs. I put on my Boston Red Sox pajamas. They were sacrilege here in the Adirondacks, Yankee Stadium was practically next door. I hated the Yankees. I said goodnight to my mother, and blew her a kiss as she turned out the light. I crawled quietly over to the window, and looked down on the porch listening for the sound of clinking beer bottles.

"How come," the nameless old man said, "every night we play this damned game, and every night nobody wins anything?" He spoke so seldom, I actually thought for some time that he was mute, or worse still, that his name was really Putz.

Uncle Morris quietly chuckled, "You putz, if you ever won, you'd probably have a coronary and then we'd have no choice but to teach Louis how this infernal game is played."

"He should spend his time thinking about girls," Mr. Kaplan said, "not playing cards with a bunch of alte kockers like us."

"Speak for yourself," my father laughed, "I'm a kocker maybe, but I'm not old yet."

As they chattered on into the night, I took my crystal radio, snapped the clip on to the radiator and fell to sleep as Yaz went two for three with a double and a long home run.

Poppy died just after Thanksgiving without much warning, and Aunt Sadie, suddenly alone, passed away early in March. Mr. Kaplan came by occasionally, for a cup of tea and a slice of pie and always told my mother what a great baker she was, although we all knew the pie came straight from the A&P over in Hadley. Once, when he thought no one was looking, he picked up the deck of Pinochle cards and stared at them fondly. That next summer, sitting on the porch of the cottage, my father taught me four new variations of solitaire.

Sophie

She has been dead for one and a half years,
for six months resting beneath the carved stone.
She lay in her bed, her memories gone,
stories of childhood lost to deafened ears,
momentary recall drowned by her fears.

I read the eulogy, my hands shaking,
recited the prayers from the time-worn draft.
Then the family gathered, many laughed
hollowly at stories I told, faking
joy, until they yielded to their aching.

I read the Kaddish in the wind-whipped rain,
then placed a shovel of dirt on her grave
and walked slowly to my car, trying to save
thoughts of the moments when she would feign
shock at something I said, but there was only pain.

Thief of Time

She was quite old,
slumping in her chair
behind the old metal desk,
her wall covered in pictures,
but none of the children.
She stole my mother
when I was not looking,
and I thought, for years,
that mothers wore white
and sat in hard backed chairs
holding bottles of formula.
She stole my name
and gave me another,
and now I have a third,
still not one of my choosing,
but one I have carried
for so many years that I
have adopted it as my own
and given it to my sons.
I asked her why she took
all that I had and she smiled
wanly, nodding, half in sleep.
I shuffled in my seat
as she looked up. It was,
she said, for the best;
she could not have cared for you
or given you what they could.
Nor can I give you what I took.
It is gone and you must accept it.
Take what you have
and give it to your sons
for they are of you,
as you were of her, and him.

She closed the file, tucked it
into the drawer and rose, slowly
straightening the ancient skirt
and touched my arm.
You look the same as you did
then, a bit older, but the same.
I can see that I acted wisely.
Think of how few can walk
these streets and see
a mother in every aging face.

Kyoto Dreams

Basho once wished he was in Kyoto
when he was sitting in Kyoto but
knowing Kyoto was also a state of mind.
When I walked around the streets in Clifden,
in the heart of Connemara, I wished
that I was Irish for I knew exactly
where I was. I was in western Ireland.
Of course, now I'm not so sure where I was
because the me who was in Connemara
had to wish that he was Irish, but
I now know from my DNA that the real
me was always part Irish,
so that real me, this me, couldn't wish
to be what he already was.
The wishing-to-be-Irish me had
to be some other me, which is
the sort of conundrum it will take
more than a few pints of Guinness
to eventually sort out. Slainte.

Circumstance

I am surrounded by circumstance. I bathe in it. It clings to me with that slightly stale odor of the apartment of every grandmother I have ever visited.

For many years I was Irish. The bodhran beat in my chest. I spoke in the trill of the Uillean pipes, the off-notes expected, accepted. Sarcasm was my drone. I would order Guinness with Indian food, with sushi. I had black hair slowly fading to white, slowly fading away. I was Black Irish.

I wrote to the adoption agency. Who am I? It was a short letter. They responded with the circumspection of another century. We can't give out names or any other identifying information, but.... I didn't want names, I wanted that loose genetic thread that I could slowly reel in, with the hope that the fish would break the surface of circumstance. I wanted a glimpse, however fleeting. I would throw it back.

Your father was a Portuguese Jew. It landed on my deck, nearly capsizing me. Your mother was possibly Sephardic, called herself sallow from her hospital bed in the maternity ward. But she was dark, absorbing the sun. That is all I can tell you. I wrote and thanked the woman from the agency. I was hungry. I wanted to eat salt cod, to sip Madeira.

A decade went by. I donated the inside of my cheek. It spoke to me. It said put on the kilt, drink the single malt, and let the pipes be Highland. And feel free to drink the Guinness as well; you have a claim to it. Suddenly I knew I wouldn't miss the salt cod. I'd been vegetarian for more than a decade.

For Giving

She gave me her time, some
of her attention, and what she
called love, and assumed it was enough.

He gave me his name, and his ever
fumbling efforts at being the father
he never had, and hoped he got close.

I'd like to say I don't begrudge
either of them, they tried, but
of course I do begrudge them both,

now both gone, and not for the children
they chose to have, though those children
did make me an outsider, but

for the self they wouldn't let me find,
my origins, for that would have
been a mortal wound to them, even

if they never said so, for an adoptee
learns quickly that you must listen with
your figurative ears to hear the true story.

I mourn them both, now, as I do
so many other friends now gone, but
my tears are saved for the parents I never knew.

At Times

At times my life suddenly opens
its eyes in the dark
and from the deepest crevices
emerge dreams that morph
into fleeting realities.

In one dark corner I have mourned
a father unknown, only likely dead,
in another one who I know is – and he
no more than a faint reflection.

Against a distant wall I dance
with my sister at her Bas Mitzvah
and not the steroid-bloated woman
eaten slowly by riotous cells
run amok through our sibling dreams.

My life abhors a vacuum
I fill it with anger
for a mother too busy trying to feed my body
while starving my soul.

I drain the puss that builds in the open sore
of a failed marriage, swab it
with the salve of a freely given love,
now feeling a love
I had never known.

It is here that I bury moments
compressed into dreams, to be dug up
another time, another place,
reborn not as artifacts, but
as precious metals.

Parentage

My second mother slipped away
without much warning, the hospital thought
she was improving, that I needn't rush there
since she'd be out in a few days,
a week at most, and four years on
there has still been no funeral.
My third father lingers, clinging
to what is left of his memories,
but happy enough in short increments,
and perhaps he too will slip away
when I am not there, and that
would be all right with me, each
time we see each other we say goodbye.
My first, and birth mother is no more
than a name and a college yearbook picture,
and a resemblance to my morning mirror image.
My second father is faded black and white
photographs and even more faded memories,
and my birth father is little more
than twisted strands of DNA
and a bit of wishful thinking.

How Do We Forgive

How do we forgive fathers?
What do you say
to a father who created you
and can't imagine your existence
or a father who held you,
smiled, and promised
the future of storybooks
and just as soon, died
on the bathroom floor,
or another father who still
remembers my name, but
for how much longer?
How do we forgive our fathers
who do not know, who
leave early and never return,
can no longer hear
what we have to say, and how
do our fathers forgive us
once they are gone?

Your Father

When they were married she
rarely spoke of him, only to him,
and all too often, by him.

After they began the divorce
all she could do was speak of him,
never to him, and he ceased

being her husband, spouse,
so he became "your father,"
as if he was a burden we had to bear.

Years after the divorce was final,
if never sufficiently so in her mind,
he remained "your father," odd

in that she said she was a widow,
her first husband having died.
But he who had been my father,

was my father no longer, just
her long dead husband, and the man
who was "your father" always

asked about her after she died,
wishing her well, never grasping
the death that was creeping up to him.

Quiet Departure

There was a quiet in the departure,
a slow leaving without any warning,
his mind an overdeveloped picture

He asked repeatedly if we were sure
it was already time for our leaving?
There was a quiet in the departure.

He forgot simple things, clung to obscure
memories, stared at his hand, at the ring,
his mind an overdeveloped picture.

It was, he said, as if his mind detoured
and once off the path, lost, his thoughts took wing.
There was a quiet in the departure.

He thought of childhood, the simple pleasure
playing on the beach, the salt water's sting,
his mind an overdeveloped picture.

He saw images he could not capture
'til he grew so tired, and just stopped thinking.
There was a quiet in the departure,
his mind an overdeveloped picture.

A Trois

Each night I crawl under the sheets
curled against the woman I love
and beside me slips your ghost.
For sixty years you were no more
than a fleeting dream, faceless, nameless,
an infrequent visitor to my gallery
of hopes, desires, and wishes.
You never had a face, did I
have one you could remember before
I was plucked from you too soon, you
lurking in the shadows of my heart.
Was I ever a child to you, in that moment
I emerged from you, or did you look away
not wanting, not daring to see a face that
still alive might haunt you through life.
Was I real in your world, in the world
into which I could never go, the world
in which no one could know I existed?
Perhaps it is fitting, mother, that you
haunt my dreams now, an apparition
locked in time by the photo I have
of you in your bloom into womanhood,
for I was a silent ghost for five decades.
But now we are reunited and, in my sleep,
you are again alive, and I now have
the woman who brought me into
the world and fled back into her own.

Still Mourning

I think about you often, lying beside
my grandparents on the hillside
overlooking the Kanawha River,
bathed in the utter silence
that only the dead can clearly hear.
I think of you more often than she
who replaced you, she who later
replaced me with her own, I
an adjacency, still useful but
no longer fully or truly valued.
I think of you lovingly, knowing
for those too few moments
my tears watered your grave,
mourning the mother I never
met but knew so well in the core
and the essence of my very being.

Apart Together

It is this time
each night
that I think of you
lying in bed,
your head pressed
deep into your pillow,
your chest rising
and falling
to an unheard beat.
I reach out for you
and grasp
the blanket
of the hotel bed
and imagine
it is your back
as I trace my finger
down the spine
of sleep.

A Perfect Stillness

You lie there, perfectly still,
the morning breeze slides away
leaving the sun to stare down,
and the birds fall into silence.

I gently touch the stone, feel
your cheek beneath my finger,
see your face, the college yearbook
photo all that I have of you.

I speak silently to you, telling
of my sixty-seven years, of your
grandsons and great grandchildren
and I sense your smile, and a tear.

Your parents are here, your
grandparents, sisters, brothers,
and cousins, and I now bring
you three generations more.

It is time for me to go, but these
moments are the most I have
of you, and as I place my small stone
atop yours, I now have a mother.

My Judas

He, the one I called brother,
wanted whatever I had
to give, a droit de
primogeniture, and I
could easily be cast aside,
a genetic other with claim
only of time, not blood.
Why did they concede to him
or were they aware?
It hardly matters now
for they are gone, she
to rest with her daughter,
he I know not where
for there was nothing
in the text message
announcing his death
as to any future resting place.
So I keep them both
in a distant corner
of my memories, he,
the self-chosen one,
who denied me any due,
I think of now only to curse
his existence on this page.

The Circus

Step right up, ladies and gents,
boys and girls, and welcome to
the New Adoption Circus.
You will be amazed at what you find,
so let the show begin right now.
In this ring, the maternal side,
you can cover your eyes and select
an adoptive mother for our host.
Will she be a traditional loving mom,
or maybe a woman agreeing to adopt
to satisfy the desires of her infertile spouse,
or just maybe she wants a child now
but imagines having her own
down the road, this one a potential
other, still family if only barely.
You never know how this will resolve.
And in the other, paternal ring,
another choice, this one easier
perhaps, a man who knows he cannot
father a child but wants a family
and will do whatever it takes,
or a man willing to accept a child,
half-orphaned at the death of his father,
who has no idea how to be a dad,
but will try and fill the role, knowing
he may father his own with
his new wife, but keeping the original,
as he promised to do at their wedding.
You've never seen a show like this,
have you, and you'll carry this one
with you for as long as you live.

Ode to a Lover

The dawn's silence was pierced
by the heron's morning chant, echoing off
the still water of the awakening lake.
He knew a moment's passion, a moment
when the universe collapsed and was
reborn anew, a little death and always
a rebirth into a world different from any
he had known before, any he would see again.
He shared the silence with his lover, with
their syncopated breathing setting
the rhythm of this day as it did
on so many other days, never knowing
what melodies would soon develop,
and carry the sun and clouds across time.
He knew this was a moment of joy, fullness
he could find nowhere else, with no one else.
He knew she made him whole, salved
the wounds time had inflicted, bathed
his soul in the sweet water of love's baptism.
In these moments he was fully alive
and knew that if there was a heaven,
it was made in the image of this day.

In the Eighth Decade

Now we choose to love in the dark,
our minds unwilling to see what
our bodies now so willingly expose.
It is not that our passion has waned
or abated, only that it has elongated
and our concept of time must be suspended.
The mind now must concede
to the heart for it understands
what the body can no longer do.
Maturity allows a depth that youth
cannot attain, desire tempered
by the body's recognition that it, too,
needs to concede to the effects of age,
and love is a cloister in which we
can still find an easy refuge.

About the Author

Louis Faber is a poet and blogger living in Florida with his wife, fellow poet Elaine Heveron and their cat, Teri. He is a retired Corporate Attorney who for several years taught Introduction to Literature at Monroe Community College. Twice adopted, thanks to DNA testing, he discovered his birth parents later in life once they had passed away. But the knowledge gleaned from the DNA testing allowed him to understand his heritage and cast a new light of many aspects of his life. He holds graduate degrees in Business Administration, a Juris Doctor and a Master of Fine Arts in creative writing. His work has appeared widely in the United States, Canada, the United Kingdom, elsewhere in Europe and Asia. He has been twice nominated for a Pushcart Prize. His first book of poetry was published by Plain View Press in 2008. His blog can be accessed at https://anoldwriter.com.

www.ingramcontent.com/pod-product-compliance
Lightning Source LLC
Chambersburg PA
CBHW070240090526
44586CB00035B/1362